THE UNITED STATES AND RUSSIAN
SPACE RACE

BY KATHLEEN COX

PEARSON

Scott
Foresman

Editorial Offices: Glenview, Illinois • Parsippany, New Jersey • New York, New York
Sales Offices: Needham, Massachusetts • Duluth, Georgia • Glenview, Illinois
Coppell, Texas • Ontario, California • Mesa, Arizona

For hundreds of years, fearless explorers, financed by great nations and empires, sought the answers to the mysteries of Earth and beyond. They sailed across oceans that extended beyond their immediate horizons. They discovered distant lands and claimed them on behalf of their kings or their queens, who wanted to expand their empires and their power. Adventurers led huge caravans far beyond **hospitable** landscapes, through barren deserts, and up and over treacherous mountain passes. They searched for bounty, from diamonds and gold to mines of **ore** rich with hidden wealth.

Some daring explorers set out on small expeditions with one goal in mind. They were determined to be the first to reach the South Pole, the first to reach the North Pole, or the first to reach the top of the world's highest peak, Mount Everest. When most places on Earth had been conquered, explorers turned their gaze upward. The next great adventure was waiting for them in space.

Explorers have conquered both Mount Everest and the moon.

To land on the moon, in particular, became the **universal** dream. The dreamers who imagined this historic event **envisioned** men tucked inside a streamlined rocket that would zoom through the Earth's atmosphere toward the lunar landscape. They were certain that mankind could get beyond Earth's gravity once they developed the right technology. It was only a matter of time.

During World War II, Germany moved this dream one step closer to reality. A team of German scientists, led by Wernher von Braun, developed the V-2 rocket. Unfortunately, the Germans weren't interested in launching this rocket into space; they used it as a missile to attack opposing countries during the war. The V-2, which was also called the Vengeance Weapon 2, was the first long-range rocket ever used in combat.

The forty-six–foot-long V-2 rocket was powerful. The Germans could program the missile so that it could hit a target two hundred miles away. The V-2 was also lethal. Its one-ton warhead could wipe out an entire city block. During the war, these rockets were aimed at London, England, where they did a lot of damage. They were also used against American and British forces advancing toward the German army.

The V-2 rocket unleashed a new kind of warfare that had never been seen before. However, the technology used to create those rockets would become a stepping-stone toward space travel.

Wernher von Braun (top) developed the V-2 rocket while a member of Germany's Nazi party. A postwar test of the V-2 rocket at White Sands missile range in New Mexico (bottom).

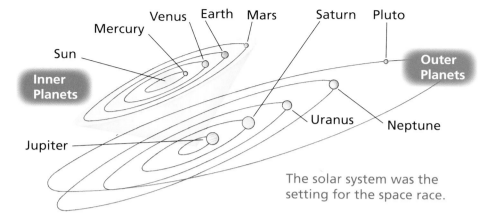

Mercury Venus Earth Mars Saturn Pluto

Sun

Inner Planets

Outer Planets

Uranus Neptune

Jupiter

The solar system was the setting for the space race.

During the war, von Braun and his scientists were members of the Nazi party, the enemies of the United States. After the war, von Braun and his team surrendered to the United States. He and some of his team members were invited to come to America, where they became citizens. In the years that followed, they worked for the army, where they developed their V-2 rocket technology to advance the military strength of the United States. Other members of the German rocket team took refuge in the Soviet Union (known today as Russia), where they helped develop the Soviet missile program.

Soon the United States and the Soviet Union, which had been allies during World War II, were in a race to develop the best technology for space exploration. They were determined to outperform each other in the race to space.

This became an important part of the Cold War. A new contest arose between the world's two superpowers—to develop the mightiest rockets. This contest would take them into the next great frontier: outer space.

There was so much to be discovered in space, and each country wanted to be the first to explore it. Planets, comets, possible **alien** life-forms, and more drove each nation to push the boundaries of science.

The space race was also an arms race, because every rocket ultimately served two purposes. A powerful rocket could fly deep into space and become the perfect vehicle for exploration, or it could be used as a missile to fire at an enemy.

On October 4, 1957, the Soviets sponsored an evening reception at their embassy in Washington, D.C. The gathering was timed for the end of a weeklong international conference on space research. Much of the discussion during the conference centered on the goal of launching a satellite into space, the first important step in space exploration.

The gathering of scientists, government officials, and members of the media heard a startling announcement. On that very day, the Soviets launched *Sputnik 1*, the world's first man-made satellite. The shiny metal sphere, which was visible from Earth, was spinning around the planet like an artificial moon. *Sputnik 1*, about twenty-three inches in diameter—the size of a beach ball—weighed 184 pounds.

It traveled about five hundred miles above Earth, at a speed of 18,000 miles per hour, and took about ninety-six minutes to circle the planet. The Soviets beat the Americans in the first leg of the space race.

The launch of *Sputnik 1*, which is shown by the model below, was celebrated with a special stamp.

This launch of *Sputnik 1* caught the world by surprise and captured the attention of the media. Until that time, the United States had been the leader in the field of technology. It had given the world electricity, the first assembly-line-produced automobile, and the first successful airplane flight. *Sputnik 1*, flying overhead, rattled Americans. Did this satellite mean that the Soviets were now the new masters of technology?

People also wondered what was actually going on inside *Sputnik 1*. Amateur radio operators could hear the satellite beeping each time it circled the Earth. What kind of information was it sending back to the Soviet Union? Could it threaten United States security? Did it have cameras on board for taking photos of secret military bases? Most frightening of all, did this satellite have small missiles on board that could be fired at American targets? As it turned out, beeping was all *Sputnik 1* could do.

About a month later, the Soviet Union launched *Sputnik 2*. This second satellite, which started orbiting the Earth on November 3, weighed about 1,120 pounds. It was much heavier than the original Sputnik. It also had a passenger: a dog named Laika, the world's first earthling in space.

This new launch proved to the world that the Soviets had the advanced technology needed to launch powerful rockets that could be a threat to the United States and its allies. Some frightened Americans compared the unexpected launch of these two satellites to the attack on Pearl Harbor.

Laika became the first earthling in space when the Soviets sent the dog up in *Sputnik 2*. The launches of *Sputniks 1 and 2* were celebrated in posters such as this one.

Слушай, страна,
Мечта людей зовет!
Сегодня твой народ
Ликует и поет.

President Dwight D. Eisenhower

After the launch of *Sputnik 2*, the United States Defense Department, which was already funding a rocket program of its own, decided to fund a more ambitious alternative program. This one would develop more powerful satellite and rocket technology. The program, named Explorer, was led by Wernher von Braun.

President Dwight D. Eisenhower, a five-star general who was supreme commander of American troops in Europe during World War II, knew that he had to restore the confidence of the American people. He understood that America's space program had to be dedicated to four clear goals that would ensure the country's advancement in the space race.

One goal was connected to mankind's urge to discover and explore the unknown. The government's second goal reflected the thinking of its successful military general. The United States needed to create a strong presence in space in order to defend the homeland and protect the nation's security.

Eisenhower's administration also recognized that the United States needed to succeed in this space race to acccomplish a third goal, that of keeping its reputation as a leader. The Cold War, an unending contest of verbal threats between the United States and the Soviet Union, was unlike any earlier conflict.

Since the arrival of television in the late 1940s, the media had played an increasingly important role in international events. People quickly became aware of the latest news, and what they saw and heard shaped their opinions of their own country and influenced their sense of security.

The final goal, determined by the Eisenhower administration, reminded Americans of another benefit from the exploration of space. By going beyond the Earth's boundaries, Americans would increase their knowledge of the universe. This knowledge would be worth a lot to the American taxpayer, who would be paying for it.

But the news about the space race remained gloomy for Americans. On December 6, 1957, American scientists finally launched their own **version** of a rocket. Called the Vanguard, it carried a satellite intended to orbit the Earth. The rocket went four feet into the air and then fell back to the ground. People called the disastrous Vanguard satellite Kaputnik.

The failure of the Vanguard rocket was front page news in 1957.

Unlike the Soviet launches, which were held in secret, the American government had invited the press to watch the take-off of the Vanguard. Everyone in the world saw the pictures of the United States' failed attempt to get into the space race. The Soviet Union used it as an opportunity to embarrass the United States at the United Nations. Soviet delegates offered foreign aid, normally given to Third World countries, to help the United States get its space program in working order.

Wernher von Braun was under tremendous pressure to succeed. In less than sixty days, the scientist and his team were ready to test their Explorer project. Late at night on January 31, 1958, the United States launched a rocket from Cape Canaveral in Florida. The rocket, with its thirty-pound satellite, called the *Explorer 1*, roared into the darkness. About two hours passed before von Braun, who was in Washington, D. C., heard a signal from the satellite. The *Explorer 1* launch was a success. The United States was finally in space. But three months after the American launch, *Sputnik 3* went into orbit. This third Russian satellite weighed more than one ton.

Eisenhower realized that his country needed a much more efficient space program. In July 1958, the president created the National Aeronautics and Space Administration (NASA). This federal agency would supervise the country's exploration of space.

The Jupiter-C rocket carried the United States' first satellite into space and put Wernher von Braun on the cover of *Time* magazine in 1958.

Everyone assumed that the country with the most successful space program would become a very powerful nation. By the end of 1958, the advantage seemed to be with the Soviets; and Americans continued to view them as a threat.

In January 1959, about fifteen months after the launch of *Sputnik 1*, the Soviets launched *Luna 1*, the first satellite destined for the moon. *Luna 1* missed its target, but it did become the first satellite to fly past the moon. Nine months later, the Soviets blasted another satellite toward the moon. *Luna 2* slammed onto the lunar surface, where it scattered memorial pendants. Each pendant was stamped with "USSR September 1959."

One month later, *Luna 3* became the world's first satellite to orbit the moon. It took the first pictures of the far side of the moon and transmitted them back to the Soviet Union. The Luna satellites were unraveling the mysteries of the strange lunar terrain. Some of it was marked with craters flooded by **molten** lava from ancient volcanoes. The lava was now solid rock.

On April 12, 1961, the Soviets once again advanced their lead in the space race when they launched a manned rocket with a space capsule. The world's first human passenger in space was Yury Gagarin. He made one full orbit around the Earth and traveled so fast that his entire flight lasted only 108 minutes. The Soviets had a new hero in their cosmonaut (the Soviet equivalent of an astronaut), and the United States had lost once again in this strange battle.

Yury Gagarin became the first person to travel in space; he gained great fame in his country and abroad.

A few weeks later, on May 5, 1961, an American Redstone rocket carried Alan Shepard Jr., America's first astronaut, into space. His journey lasted only fifteen minutes before he splashed down into the Atlantic Ocean near Bermuda, but the astronaut boosted America's sagging spirits. The United States had its first space hero. Shepard was honored with an enormous ticker-tape parade in Washington, D.C.

By 1961, America also had a new president, John F. Kennedy. Three weeks after Shepard's historic flight, the president challenged his country in a speech before Congress to land a man on the moon and bring him safely back to Earth, before the end of the decade. Kennedy's speech put the Soviet Union on notice and raised the spirits of his fellow Americans.

Congress committed billions of dollars to Kennedy's Apollo lunar-landing project. But America's scientists wondered if they could meet the President's deadline and beat the Soviets, who were also racing to land a man on the moon. This was the milestone that really mattered to each country.

President Kennedy presents a medal to Alan Shepard Jr., who became the first American in space aboard the *Freedom 7*.

Astronaut Scott Carpenter trains at Langley Air Force Base in 1962.

American astronauts learned how to operate their own spacecraft and the special lunar vehicle that would get them on and off the moon. They learned how to conduct scientific experiments that would enrich the country's knowledge about space and their lunar destination.

Each astronaut also endured punishing physical training so that he could withstand the speed of the rocket journey that would hurl him through the Earth's atmosphere and far into space. The astronauts also had to learn to work in a state of weightlessness, in which their bodies, along with their space tools, would float freely around the space cabin.

Because the capsule that would return to Earth could go astray, the astronauts learned how to survive in a jungle, in a desert, on a mountain, or in the middle of the ocean. These explorers showed superior intelligence and physical strength. Even though all the astronauts would be highly qualified and well prepared for their role in space, only the best would be chosen to make the journey.

This postcard depicts Valentina Tereshkova, the first woman in space, and other Soviet cosmonauts.

Scientists and engineers also had to solve enormous technical problems. They had to design space suits so that the astronauts could survive outside the spacecraft and on the moon. They had to create a complicated lunar vehicle that would land the astronauts on that distant, unfamiliar surface. They had to design the powerful spacecraft that would get the astronauts beyond Earth and into space and then bring them back home.

In August 1961, about three months after President Kennedy's speech, the Soviets launched another cosmonaut into space. Gherman Titov circled the Earth for about twenty-five hours. Shepard's flight had lasted only fifteen minutes.

In the middle of 1963, the Soviet Union achieved another first that grabbed the world's attention. They rocketed the first woman into space. Cosmonaut Valentina Tereshkova orbited the Earth for three full days before she parachuted back into Soviet territory and landed her place in history.

But America's space program was moving forward. After much discussion, scientists decided on the most suitable spaceship to get a man to the moon. The spacecraft would have enormous power and size, so that it could break through Earth's atmosphere, beyond Earth's gravity, and cruise into space. Along the way, the rocket would discard sections that had performed their task like a **barge** unloading freight at different points.

Once the spacecraft escaped Earth's gravity and was headed on its course to the moon, the streamlined rocket would be free of all unnecessary weight that could slow down its journey. The spacecraft would also be designed to split into two modules, or sections, after it began to circle the Moon. One section was the lunar module that would carry two astronauts to the Moon. The command module, which contained the instruments to return the astronauts to Earth, would remain in lunar orbit.

While scientists designed all this complicated technology and the astronauts learned how to use it, the two rival powers continued to launch cosmonauts and astronauts into space. They had to test the new procedures and the new technology that would move each country closer to the finish line, where a man would stand on the moon.

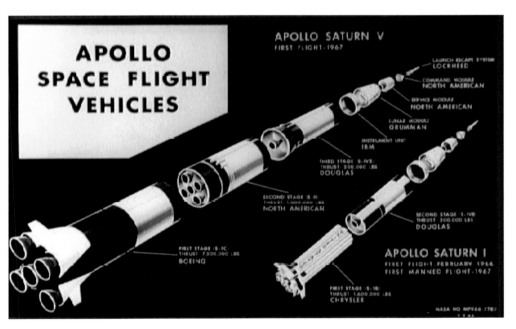

In October 1964, the Soviet Union put three cosmonauts into space. But they were forced to return early. The Soviet premier, Nikita Khrushchev, was forced to retire from his position. This left the government unstable for a time.

The new leader, Leonid Brezhnev, showed his commitment to the space effort and authorized the next rocket launch, which led to the first space walk in 1965. It was a quick, ten-minute walk outside the ship, but the Russians claimed another victory.

Five days after the space walk, the United States launched two astronauts, Gus Grissom and John Young, into space aboard their *Gemini 3* spacecraft, which they dubbed the *Molly Brown*. The astronauts were in complete control of their flying machine as it made three orbits around the Earth.

In June, America launched the *Gemini 4* spacecraft, which also carried two astronauts. One of them, Ed White, took a twenty-minute walk in space. The two astronauts orbited the Earth for ninety-seven hours and fifty-six minutes, setting an American record. During the next Gemini flight, two astronauts stayed in space for eight days. This was the world's longest piloted flight to date.

In future months, more American flights awed and inspired the world. In December 1965, two flights, *Gemini 6* and *Gemini 7*, linked up in space. The two crews talked as their separate spacecrafts floated about a foot apart from one another. *Gemini 7* went on to stay in orbit for nearly two weeks. The long flight proved that astronauts could endure the trip to and from the moon.

In December 1968, the United States launched *Apollo 8*, the first manned space mission to circle the moon and return safely to Earth. A few months later, the Soviets successfully landed two unmanned vehicles, called lunar rovers, on the moon. They explored the lunar surface and analyzed rock and soil deposits. Each country was barreling forward in the race to make Kennedy's deadline.

On July 16, 1969, the world witnessed the launch of *Apollo 11*, which carried three American astronauts: Neil Armstrong, Edwin "Buzz" Aldrin Jr., and Michael Collins. They were on their way to the moon. Collins steered the control module as it went into lunar orbit. Armstrong and Aldrin pulled on their space suits and crawled into their lunar module. They separated from the command module and descended to the moon.

When the lunar module finally touched down on July 20, 1969, the first manned spacecraft from the Earth was on the moon. Hours later, Armstrong stepped onto the surface. A television camera and microphone on the lunar module recorded the moment and the words that he said: "That's one small step for a man, one giant leap for mankind."

To the far left, astronauts James McDivitt (near) and Ed White are shown inside the *Gemini 4* spacecraft; near left is a photo of the detached capsule of *Gemini 7*.

Buzz Aldrin (inside the circle) stands next to the American flag during the *Apollo 11* mission. Later missions, such as *Apollo 17,* explored other areas of the moon using lunar rovers.

Following the example of explorers discovering new lands, Armstrong and Aldrin planted the American flag. Then they collected rocks and soil samples for scientists to study back on Earth. They set up sensors to record vibrations caused by moonquakes and performed other important experiments. Then they climbed back into their lunar module.

Three hours later, the two astronauts docked with the command module, which would take the crew back home to public adoration and world acclaim. These American astronauts had realized mankind's ancient dream.

The leaders of the Soviet Union and the United States knew that man's first lunar landing represented an astonishing accomplishment.

During the next few years, the two countries turned their attention toward the creation of space stations and space laboratories that would float in orbit above the Earth. The Soviets launched their first space station, called *Salyut 1*, in 1971. In 1973, the United States launched Skylab, a space station that was designed to house a small number of astronauts and their experiments over an extended period of time.

Slowly, hostilities began to die down between the United States and the Soviet Union, and the two countries began to **refrain** from competing with each other. In 1975, the two countries decided to take part in a joint project. They would dock two manned spacecraft together up in space. The meeting took place on July 17. For nearly two days, the crews from the rival countries visited, ate meals together, and put together two pieces of a commemorative plaque that celebrated the occasion.

During this mission, when the U.S. Apollo spacecraft and the Soviet Soyuz spacecraft docked in orbit around the Earth, the world saw how the technology that had once held the two countries apart now brought them together.

Astronaut Deke Slayton and cosmonaut Aleksey Leonov meet in orbit.

Glossary

alien *n.* a creature or object from outer space.

barge *n.* a large, strongly built vehicle or flat-bottomed boat for carrying freight.

envisioned *v.* pictured in your mind.

hospitable *adj.* friendly; receptive.

molten *adj.* made liquid by heat; melted.

ore *n.* a rock containing enough of a metal or metals to make mining profitable. After it is mined, ore must be treated to extract the metal.

refrain *v.* to keep yourself from doing something.

universal *adj.* of or belonging to all; concerning all.

version *n.* one particular statement, account, or description.